BECOMING
EDIBLE

ISBN Paperback: 979-8-9904500-0-4

ISBN Hardcover: 979-8-9904500-1-1

ISBN E-book: 979-8-9904500-2-8

BECOMING EDIBLE

ANNE WESLEY JONES

everything, always, for my mother

CONTENTS

ROADKILL REIMAGINED

At the edge
of myself
there is always an animal
waiting
for contact,

and it does not matter
whether or when I blink; I see it
lean and pacing or
crouched and camouflaged,
a coiled spring
with curling breath
of an exhale smoking
or crystalline misting
icy clear. It doesn't matter
whether in her animal body she is
baring teeth and
shallow breath whiffling
the feather-scrapped-together cape,
floppy wings made shift
from the first receiving blanket
thin and shivering—
the animal is
always doing what an animal does
to stay alive.

Yesterday I traveled
372 miles
behind a wheel
steering 6,000 pounds
of plastic and metal,
machine rolling on a road
through scrub and sage
and on to fields and fields
of sunflowers,
and I saw them,
all of them,
their bodies:
the armadillo,
three skunks,
a hare,
two raccoons,
the front half of a deer,
and what meat remained
of unnamable flesh
when the turkey vultures
would wing skyward
just before I barreled by,
75 miles behind me
every hour.

It didn't matter
for them, either,
what they were doing
at the edge
of the road.

It wasn't enough.
And I wonder
what might have been,
what might be
possible
at slower speeds
for the armadillo, yes,
and the rabbit, raccoons,
even the skunks,
but also for me.

Survival, surely,

and
if I slow enough
(how much is enough?),

trust

between that wild body,
wired with instinct
to live
at all costs,
and this wandering
self,
the landscape surveyor
penciling in placenames,
measuring distances
out from the center,
all the miles traversed and marking

the boundaries of longing,
this marrow seed yearning
to call everyplace
home.

I

OFF LEASH

SPRINGTIDE

i.

The wind, out and all around,
is picking up again,
brisk enough to polish bone,
so weigh anchor!
Hoist the sail!
Now is the time
to split the breeze.

ii.

Spring forever unfurls
the realm of youth
where rainbows flicker in sneezes,
and wafts of cigarette smoke
carry the scent of hope
after a downpour
at a Valero.

iii.

Today the dandelion
leafs its way up my doorstep,
unfolding
tang for the tongue
and yellow tendrils
dripping into a bullseye:
the budding season.

iv.
Without, the fickle winds;
within, pythoness uncurls,
stretching up
exuberant, yawning
along the spine,
hitching equinox to solstice,
sunning herself.

v.
Red robin's song,
robust and bright, rings
morning and evening, now
its breath rushing along
Earth's tilt, the loudest oracle
of divine
opportunity.

BLACK AND SAFFRON

Singing requires voice,
dragonflies four wings for flight.
Lightning bugs
strike, firing the night,
trail humid artichoke afterprints
mossy behind the eyelids:
original courage foreordained.

The Earth herself knows
about time's illusion,
relativity, and revolution.
She sees our hovering
suspension leaning unseasonal,
a trembling withdrawal
from pendulous Gravity and his force,
and she sees
      our cautious arousal
toward awareness
of truth: that his unbearable
weight and universal laws
have already been rendered
as insubstantial

as the Monarch's
black-and-saffron
memory
of her crawling days,

since chrysalis released
to migratory momentum, humming
single wing flaps, each
filling unsummable space
with dogged movement
vertical, northward,
exhaling open vowels
on the windward return.

GROWING UP

Some Sunday visitors were solemn,
wafer-thin and watered down,
but not so this one,
arriving brightly sheathed
before dawn,
rainy day nestled in thin plastic
or sunny, rubber-banded on the lawn,
rolled up and waiting
to be brought in, unfolded.

Sunday was the full-color spread
of mini stories, so many
to choose from and all of them
single-minded, purpose only to incite
a smile. What chuckling jollyhood!
What silly nonsense! Delight
to decipher this collection of codes,
a neural pathway from anticipation to
humor
one panel at a time,
one speech bubble, one word—this
language, image, and then
laughter.

And more! the joyful economy! of how
later, saved and snipped

no matter the ink rubbing off, the papers
could be nobly repurposed
as collages and bookmarks and
birthday party present wrapping
and wadded up kindling
beneath the fireplace woodpile.

Flat-out magic.

Darling, now maybe
you see
this
is why
I've been holding on
tighter, longer
than I probably should,
than I know
that we know that I ought to,
because

I'm not sure when I stopped
hopping breakfast tableside,
impatient for the gumming-up news and ads
to be shucked from the funnies
so I could gleefully flee with them
to some under-bed hiding place,
rolling and giggling and slurping up
the setups and punchlines.
I don't even know—was I seven? five
years old? twelve,

with telescoping legs and a lopsided chest?
When Archie and Blondie and Snoopy and Dennis
and the boy with the tiger
and the family with too many kids to keep straight
quit holding my attention, lost
it, the baked-bread-with-sugar-sweet
Sunday sensation.
But it was
all of a sudden
flattened, and then it was gone,

a room that vanished
behind a shutting door.

DEAR CAROL,

Did I ever know your last name?
I suppose
that wasn't important
for sneaking off
to arrange our stacked firewood fort,
play house behind the sheet,
discarded shower curtain
tucked in between the scrap-board slots
we'd lain carefully
crosswise above corner-fence pickets,
those sharp sentries
marching in at the right angle
to protect a tiny triangle of privacy.

We would traipse adventuring
up and down the alleys,
discovering
a broken toilet seat beside the dumpster,
cream-colored and padded and perfect
for permanent marking
"Home Sweet Home," hanging on the nail
six foot, too high up for me to reach,
so you hung it, our front-door wreath.

Sometimes your brothers would try
to join us, but they never knew
how, didn't play by the rules,

always attacking—"pew pew"—
pretend projectiles crashing around,
splattering into the invisible soup
I was very busy stirring.
They'd finally leave us
to the task of tidying
their casings, long since smoking,
and we'd lob them back
over the fence for them to find,
lock, and load
another day.
It was always after
we were supposed to have come in
for dinner, pink sky and pushing our luck,
the minutes were bubbles
with swirling soap rainbows
inside that moment behind the white drape,
when one of us would ask
or suggest or remind,
casually, no big deal,
but perched at the cliff's edge
of every paused breath
electric and tingling,
"Want to do that one thing again?"
where you'd lift your t-shirt, unlatch
the hook-and-eye fastening, and give us both
the simultaneous sensation of moistening
in our mouths, and elsewhere,
as my fingers found budding breasts
in this girlish act, innocently

foreshadowing
the best of womanhood:

Invite, reveal, delight.

CROW CONVERSATIONS

My mother's voice has the lean of gossip
when she discloses a secret fear:
"We think Momma might have been
a lesbian."
She leverages collective suspicion,
the kind of snowball authority
daring a spitting challenge
so she can roll out her arsenal of evidence:
sixty-year-old memories
of supervising her sisters in the car while
their mother went in, more than once
and for what seemed like hours,
to the closed-up home of the spinster
with the reputation.

In answer, I imagine their little-girl bodies
climbing over tufted leather seatbacks,
floorboard-hiding, push-pulling
with slender fingers the thunking latches—
down, locked; up, unlocked—
in repetitive play of power
reflected in the quarter glass,
unfolding outward to vent the impatience
that would calcify with age
into infamy.
And probably the women were
making love, and I imagine

hearing two soft voices entwining
like the steam from their teacups,
rising to touch across the table
where knowing gazes met
and held each other, sharing space,
where a stovetop kettle and a box of tissues
comprised a chrome kitchen refuge,
brief and intermittent,
from the domestic duties waiting
out front, in the car
and beyond.
And even though, for my mother,
redemption would require more
than my offering response
of yard-watching my daughters
run and tumble in the petaled dusk,
tilting into familiar figures of starlight
together,
it is what I have, so
I invite her.

TWO DOGS
for Molly

This morning
when the sky was oranging
itself into light, and the trees and
traffic signals sprouted grackle crowns,
I saw two dogs in two cars,
both front-seated:
one lapside

behind the wheel
and cradled by its mistress,
who was attempting a left turn
around oncoming cars, rush hour;
the other I glimpsed rearview
wearing long ears
and a smile.

I was moving fast
between the lines, blurry
lane stripes rumbling along, but
in that instant I felt their warm muscle
leaning toward me, soft breath,
and concomitant delight
to be moving, too.

SUNDAY AFTERNOON IN THE
DAVIS MOUNTAINS
(formerly known as Las Limpias, and now lost
to their long-past people's known names)

Have you heard?
If you lean in, peer close
to the print, I will show you
a constellation of sounds
layering this sensate world
right now.

First there is a whooshing,
valvular momentum
on regular repeat;
the intervals point
to the medial, central
deep beat
that crosses the crisp tip
of the needle: head of pin
holding both worlds.

This near, there is also the breath
like sand shifting steeply downhill,
swish-following thick footprints,
plus the ticktock of the wristwatch
click-clacking, start-stopping
time
outside of rhythm.

Then is the fly's circus tumbling,
staccato intermittent scribbling
its wild cursive in the air.
A companion clears his throat,
a rumbling sighing sound,
while the sparrow
on the ponderosa perches,
pink throat piping pointed arrows,
verbal fireworks,
with puckered tips of sparklers
dissolving on the wind.

Somewhere nearby is a rustling
like breeze-loved leaves, sun yellowing
or a foraging nose, some muzzle
rummaging or bark-scraping or
creeping feet or hooves or flank, maybe,
rubbing the stiff tufts of golden grass
sprung up among the sotol
and the desert holly.
The ice, almost silent,
melts, creaking in the cooler.

And the hum, choral pulse
two junipers and a cottonwood away,
must be bees, or at least hundreds of wings
with such buzzing velocity
the ear bones can feel
its drumming voice
exactly this far
across the hollow.

In a shadowed crag above here,
a bird spills a melody, laughter splashing
down the rocks like water,
and greets the chirping voice
of an unnamed insect announcing
the spreading of dusk.

Beyond this copse, in the gravel lot
half a mile away
thumps the shut of a door,
and beyond there
the cars curdle air currents
with their concrete haste,
whispering over a windy echo
to our camp chairs, their metal frames cooling
in the stretching shadows.

Listen, that's it. You must
remember
how to lean in close
to the moment, the one
that keeps unfolding.

It is generous, unparalleled
in lending itself, no matter what
to be held
in your awareness, its offering
mutual, expansive,
directionless, an endless
window of attention
always opening
to radiant being.

DEAR KARA K—,

I fell in love with you that day
after having flirted
with the idea, blushing
when our shoulders brushed
each other's, carefully
considering the sculpted spirit
Menos by Hans Van de Bovenkamp,
as our poetry class paraded around campus
tasked with ekphrasis.

I wondered about you,
whether it had been the same
when you left your own home
for this education.
Maybe you knew as well as I
what it was to have a childhood
punctuated by the occasional shadows
of semi-present parental figures,
blossoming into focus
about as often as springtime.

Maybe you, too, had renounced
a climate of arid earth, of crackling skin,
brittle hair blowing like bare branches
foregrounding the flattest horizon.
I'd traded the Northern Plains,
prone to drought,
for the Brazos watershed and

for me, the plunge into the deep end
of autonomy
was shockingly humid, dripping
with sweaty social blunders
like the first time I went through with it,
sex,
willingly, *bravely*, I'd thought,
and still he had to ask me
not to just lie there
beneath him
as if I knew any other way.

I never did get used to
the moisture in the air,
how it tried, oh so gently,
to convince my body
to relax.
With a dewy touch for dry eyes
it could coax curls into my hair,
play its soft strokes, and
bathe my skin, plump, swelling
wet,

like it had its own ideas,
agendas,
which I took to be nothing short of
pleural effusion.

But that day in May, it was sultry hot
and I was walking home, ricocheting
across the academic plaza
when our gazes met,
our smiles echoed,
and our laughter rang out—
a counter curse dispelling self-doubt.
I was carrying my pillow, redeemed
from its place in his bed
where I had already relearned
how to collapse
in on myself.

That day, you were witness
to an all-out rescue mission:
my very first.

WITHIN UNLOOKED-FOR PLACES

In this blessing,
the tracks are light
and the way is led
by an ant,
by sow bugs and flies,
springtails, pre-beetles
grubbing among the radishes
and beetroots
and rot.

There are also bodies
of memories
buried here
where turnips and topsoil
press warmingly together
with sifting whispers.

Meanwhile, the flame is scraping
the underbrush above,
charcoaling every boundary
of the trail,
smearing its black secret
molecular-rendering
truth:

this vision
of unbecoming.

It is thermal time, movement
in the singular direction
without end,
its rhythm silent
and so slow to be
beneath sight or hearing
of the living.

Here it does
its undoing:
untying tendons,
unlashing ligatures
of flesh to mind,
of things
that happened
that hurt.

This is a blessing way
with no carving
or cord-cutting;
there is no severance,
no storage,

only a sweet smell,
a dissolution
gently sorting
the harrowed crumbs
huddling together
anew, again,
to hug the carrot hairs,

those branching fibers,
with a promise
of bright-orange root
for being
itself
for the squirrel
and the rabbit,
for your table.

II

POINTING

AFFECTIVE DISORDER
(HIGH HOLY DAYS)

Here it is, the guest of the season
I've been avoiding.

It is sad,
so, so sad.

It is an underworldly sorrow,
a keening, lamenting thing,
an exposed tooth root,
raw nerve in the mouth
that cannot be soothed
or held gently enough for relief,
that won't be
comforted until
lights out—the body is left
altogether.

No wonder why
I try to keep my door locked
against its shuddering entreaty.
It has no body
to care about
convenience and demands
to be wept,
eclipsing everything.

The poets might promise
something like joy or freedom
on the other side of this
suffering, but I swear to God,
if someone quotes Leonard Cohen
at me, I will lose it
altogether.

Just like that, the guest
has me
pinned to this moment.
So here we are, then,
reluctant companions:
me praying the world will keep orbiting
the sun, who sees
the sorrow begging
me to stay with it,
and my chickenshit commitment
to try.

DEAR LISA M—,

More than a decade later, I think
I can tell you the truth:
It was your voice
that sent me fleeing
to hide under the bed
one sophomore night in college
at twenty years old,
where the space between the box springs
and the carpet dust compresses,
flimsy foxhole
undignified.

That's what fear does, I guess:
extracts
dignity.

There was my terror
at seeing the mirror of your face
in the same room as my new boyfriend's
memory, which still harbored
the scent of your hair hanging over him,
the shape of your rising nipple,
or
only the two of you knew what else.

And not because I'd heedlessly
discarded my mother's warnings,

dropped the shield of my panties
for him,
letting him balloon himself
into the folds atop my thighs,
a childish sensation
piercingly familiar.

(it's easy to give up what's already been taken)

And anyway, I always knew
the panties had never been anything
more than a charm, rabbit's foot,
implausible amulet.

When I was seven and would play
hide-and-seek, I could dive
beneath the bed, swift motion rolling
all the way to the center,
utterly unseeable—
almost.

When you sauntered into his apartment
after your vacation, surveying the territory
I was laying claim to,
I had to belly-scoot
feet and bottom first,
flattening my flesh,
releasing the air from my lungs to fit,
and twisting my neck, turning my head,
field of vision restricted

to the slight shaft of light angling in
from the hallway where your laughter,
seeking me out,
was unmistakable.

Most kids would agree
the game doesn't end until
everyone's discovered,
but yours was a high-stakes advance,
and my terror
was of the predatory probing
roving ready-or-not claw of a feeling,
this finally having something worth protecting—

not the folds, or what did or didn't happen there,
but through the passage past their gate
upward, inward, in toward the heart,
where I'd let him spark
this new tantalizing,
achingly delicate sensation:
belief
and its accompanying wonder.

TRAFFICKING

Welcome, welcome fairies,
elves, duendes, dwarfs,
spirits of the liminal,
attendants to the straight-up hairs
on the back of my neck,
and the soft-falling sandcastle space
in between dreams.

Yes, yes, I know you
have a frolicking love
for mischief
just like the jumping spider
at a crowded poolside in summer,
or the autumn wind in bright sunshine
sneaky and chilling under the collar,
like the mid-sentence app crash,
the mold on the muffins,
the now-empty urn
covered in kids' stickers
and marked up with their names,
like me.

I might as well
settle in for the visit
since in the pit of my stomach I sense
your approach after sunset,
compressing the veins in my forearms,

wrists, and the backs of my hands,
and the only thing to do
is nail them down,
palms up, to the wood
and wait.

Come anyway, won't you,
with your sweet siren call
dripping temptation, poorly
disguised as white lies?
A wrapped candy trail
leads to a place I know
not worth revisiting
because I trust you
to leave
like you always do
in the morning,
your glistening gifts
of dew on the web
reflecting rainbows and stories
of sorrow and valor
and friendships that hold
with steel-silky strength
absolutely
worth, every time, the retelling.

Welcome back a short while,
little diggers of psyche,
pyros, and storm crows,
you pixie, imp, goblin, gnome.

There's room for you, too,
in my twiggy night crown
of snakes and spines
and eight-legged weavers.

And when you do
depart, be gone!
Have done with it!
On your way out, you might,
if you care to,
take with you
these tiny cheesecloth-wrapped tokens:
a chocolate, a coffee,
smoke blown out the window,
a bottle of wine, a phone call avoided,
and some old moldy muffins.
Here. They're all lined up and left
on the porch, front doorstep of mind,
even as such, these some sort
of my
thanks.

ONE PRAYER FOR SOLSTICE

The beginning may be
before
memory
of the ear-buzzing admonitions,
choral chants, tinnitus whines,
to hold your mouth steady
open
that a nut, wandering seed,
fruit might fall
happenstance
to the tongue
half-hidden by teeth,
or maybe cricket-jump
upspringing into a limp palm,
or when the wind is generous,
flick it between parted lips,
sweet thrill and satisfying
the hunger
dark and urgent,
to keep the body clean
of the procuring
of pleasure.

At the window, outside,
a horse fogs the glass
between you.

Nearby, the figure in the kitchen
casts a soft shadow
with her well-muscled forearms
and skillful whisking fingers,
unties the baking twine—
a knotted, fraying bridge between
what tastes good
and transgression.
The bread is tended to,
the figure kneading
what will rise.
Stars peek out the past,
the moon wanes,
and night lengthens.

Your windpipe
and esophagus
hold each other,
embracing.

An oily, twiggy hand
is reaching
up from deep within, below
the belly
toward your neck,
its grip curling and rooty,
and when you pry and pull
it out, weeding it up
through the center,
its trailing hairs

alive with fury
and its polyp tail
of squealing infants
come up with it.

The horse whinnies.
You cough,
sore and wheezing.

She lights a lamp, knowing
with what care
new pairings must be made:
something to soothe
and strengthen,
flavors creamy and piquing
aside of what's safe,
salty sustenance, familiar
grain leaf stalk
onion pear lentil
breast hip wing
bone song rhythm.
She is laughing, joyful,
when you ask her
to prepare your meal.

You open
the window.
The horse leans in,
watching you stir
and pour and simmer and tidy

and you hear,
loud at close listening,
both its breath
and its heartbeat.

TRUE STORY

She will shed her flesh and feathers
in the end,
underground,
and still fly,
hollow bones strung together
with a deeper magic
than what stirs the sea above
or ripples the mudbrick road
beneath, and down further,
this place
where we are
traveling in the starless night.

My raven mother will,
when called on,
accompany me—
a pilgrim, stranger—
where she knows the way,
although she is displeased
about the skeleton passport
required for attendants
this far in
dreams and visions,
where shanty oaths lean
slippery
over uncollected fragments

of the self
that loiter, congregating.

We've come for you.

We both know
there is a pleasure in clenching
that has come here to die,
that cool, dulling satisfaction,
a black-mirror smoke signaling,
a closed fist,
a meteor approaching,
frozen gasp
long past expiration,
alluring and elusive, fingers grasping
around the curling wisps
and not even a heliograph,
just empty air.
Exhale.

Now the girl with the knives
bubbles up from below,
alive with a wild laughter,
falling in sparkles
ringing around her temples,
eyes shining, a twinkle
of conspiracy.
She will light a fire
under us all.

And
you've been telling lies
about her. Yes.

"Yes, and so have we."
The fragments slink forward
in shadow, creeping
toward the truth
which is part confession,
part howling question
about forgiveness.
And the raven speaks
about doorways
and the wind blows
and the fire burns
and someone is dancing.
The girl puts down her knives,
and from somewhere above
it is snowing.

She gestures with her head,
the winged one,
and the snowflakes go still,
suspended,
and she gives me a choice
and I choose to go home
blindfolded, waking
to the promise of sunrise
and with cobwebby dreams
of dancing bones.

FOR A STRANGER

the welcome
is the beginning
of shedding dread,
of being found
deficient.

*

She is back
in my dreams,
the one body
of water
that encircles the planet.
also my mother is there,
watching her own waist
like she does,
and sometimes there's another,
maybe my uncle—father's brother—
or my brother's wife, and
always in vaguely known places
mythic and half remembered:
coastal Georgia, the Yucatán,
a Hawaiian island.

also you are there,
among us, the dogs
at the children's chins

and them at our heels
dashing and squealing,
the salad plates needing carrying
to the sink and then the washing
and swimsuits needing finding and
the landlady, hotel hostess,
fanning "fun for the whole family" flyers
under our noses
as you and i sit close
on the open-air patio
shoulder to shoulder,
smiling
at the bustle, its chaos and noise
slightly ridiculous
when we can feel it,
and by *it* I mean Her,
how She waits for us
just across the next strip of sand,
asking for our feet
so She can hold our toes,
heels, ankles,
us.

more often, though, i am on the boat,
the crowded ferry
hot with humans
and low in the water,
narrowly missing scraping
the canal walls, water-stained
and hemming in

the way—forward motion only,
sight obscured by bodies
overleaning toward us,
and passengers
sagging below the limp sunshade
strung up on splintering poles,
and all of us being steered
in the single-most direction:
onward.

in these dreams you are beside me,
but i am remembering
the first time,
high on the mountain,
that our eyes met,
unafraid
of each other's, mirroring
our own, and
what's more,
silkworm spinning
a liquid line between us.

i seem to have swallowed it,
this thread,
and in the alchemy of my belly
it becomes a buoy.

welcome,
traveler. welcome,
weaver of dreams. welcome,
seer. i hope: companion.

and even gripping
tight, trying
to trust memory,
the chores by day and
sleep adventures melt
into each other. molting
is a process, and how do you say
i love you
in a straight-line language
when She, the Sea
who must be
holding us all,
knows nothing
of borders?

maybe we can meet
in an estuary.

and
waiting
is also living.

DEAR JANET MCCANN,

It's intimidating, starting a conversation
with a real poet, but I have to
beg your pardon, pry. Besides,
I remember you were encouraging,
unfazed by hundreds of students'
sour complaints and machinations,
endless and shifty, of academia, so
one little poem
must be small beans
to you.
I know we corresponded once
a long time ago (it seems
to me), but
I forgot your address (how could I
never have written
it down?), and I will confess
I creeped, combing the internet
trying to find it, staving off panic
every time my search for your name
yielded someone else's
obituary.

So if it's not too much,
I'd like to hear,
peering backward, poking around attic corners
of your mind, forty years professing
on saint-like contemplation and women

writers, can you instruct
how much
must we make peace
with our pasts, ourselves, and
how?
I ask because
I heard you are concerned
about feral cats and
the others among us that are
similar, and because I see you
as a sage.

"Crone," too, self-designated (I
haven't read it yet, your newest book,
but I like to imagine you gambling,
recounting winnings: sunburnt summers
of children's laughter splashing
like city water from rubber-green hoses
into sagging backyard pools hosting
grass trimmings, primary occupants,
or
discovering the victory of flying the white flag
first
at breakfast-table battles, capitulation
a savvy maneuver when exercised daily
for realigning alliances
in a lengthening marriage,
or
how many times
you forgave your mother;

did you?), could offer clues
into my future, unapologetic
woman.

I'm asking for navigation tips
around motherhood's muddy waters,
where
kicked-up silt keeps hiding inevitable nets
of demand, contradiction—how to be working
my way upstream
with the echo of the ocean in my mind
and still carrying young, clinging
dreams of maybe actually being
enough after all
if only
I steer clear
of gossip and measuring tape,
and giving up: the hooks luring
the last catch, cleavers waiting
at the end of the line.

Tell me, how did you manage
to avoid getting closed up within,
flower-pressed between
the pages of someone else's story?
I need to know. How do you hold
the pen and still skirt the sticky ink
smear-staining the body
mirror-words
of dates and directions, deadlines

leaked from a calendar
planner, the timekeeping record
I thought I could claim as a shield,
but was only paper thin
all along, easily torn?

Please, dear Janet, Emerita, do
try to be honest with me, and
if you, in your scholarship or meditations, found
the secret, share it: how
to let go
that grip on the war gear, grave clothes,
to let surround the sounds
of now,
this,
the only moment.

A PLAINS PERSON SINGING,
HOMEWARD BOUND *for William Washington*

Thirty miles from Raton
in New Mexico's northeast corner,
at Capulín, the chokecherry has all but vanished
from the outer slopes.
There is a gated entry and a paved trail
leading into the crater
and at the center, near the ancient vent
now strewn with basalt cinder bombs
and their clinging lichen gowns,
with rocks adorned by prickly poppy
and the "lover of disturbed
areas," the yellow cowpen daisy,
the chokecherry still abounds.
Standing in the center
of the bowl, with the crater walls
steep and inward sloping,
I notice
how the juniper and pinion pines
have taken hold
of the earth in this place
in a noisy embrace,
needling the ears in the spiraling wind.

"Feel that? Pause and pay attention!"
someone said to me this week—
a stranger lately, now a friend,

Will—of the wind. So I do,
listening to the blue flax and thistles
announcing themselves,
ushered by their own voices
into this moment,
knowing their rights
to be here.

Around the rim, a mile-long loop
unfolds hundred-mile views,
and in an eyeful and a moment in my mind,
I can interstate travel.
It's hard to hear anything
above the whoosh-shushing noises
across the low brambling, the twisted trunks
and roots cleaving sidelong to the soil,
but when I pause at the lonely peak,
out of breath and burning at the lungs and thighs
with only the sky above me, and maybe
briefly a red-tailed hawk—or
perhaps it is a turkey vulture?—
I am suddenly, rushing air and all,
somehow home. I am aware
I don't belong, not quite
like the raven and the roadrunner,
the mountain jay who keeps appearing
in my dreams and who was certainly called
something else
by the Haisndayin—
the people "who came from below"

and reverent crossed this land,
overwintering here

alongside the pronghorn
and the mule deer and the bighorn sheep,
taking refuge from the northern winds
on the flatlands the buffalo stayed for
long before the Spanish
came, carrying a naming power
that stuck
to Capulín itself,
long before pink-skinned people
came with coins and cattle,
fences and gates and
the National Monument placards,
assertively measuring out
this paved rim path.

And even now, there is a summit sense
of the sacred, this holy mystery.
It is all here
across time, together
a lingering story, a ghosting legacy
that defines this place, and
I am looking down into the crater
at la boca, the vent, the place of eruption,
and I see
how it is
still
some kind of shelter.

AT THE OCOTILLO

It is a wet whip,
red-tipped ribbon
waving, reaching
with whipping embrace
offered to pilgrims,
crossing the cracks
turned to fissures
on this concrete crossroad,
past abandoned gas stations
sitting sun-bleached
and watery with heat.

The sage grass stays
to watch, to bear witness
with the prickly pear
paddle-clapping
in celebration
of your coming,
if you will
discover what happens
here,
kneeling and bared
before its spiny long arms,
its wild flagellations,
windless thrashings,
silence.

It doesn't matter whom
you meet within,
which ones rise
in response
to the lonely cactus call.
It matters only that you meet them:

The one that crouches, cringing,
wailing, "No, no, no,"
over and over;
the one
who regrets
coming, wishing for home;
the ones who fail
to return
your gaze; and the ones
who are reckless
with guns
and words
and water.

That you meet them
and stay
long enough
to hold wide the door
for their entry
to your heart, wet as the song
of the scrub sparrow
with the black throat—
until, beneath new moon

in starlight,
you see their patterns,
constellations of winged shadow
you hoped would never be,

and you begin
to whisper them
together,
home again.

If you do not run now,
you will find
the pathway back
lined with tufts of lavender,
an undulating chorus
of greeting
along with regal attendants
sistering new worlds
at sunrise
with their business
of giving
gifts
of pollen
and striped flight.

BILDUNGSROMAN

Sitting on his lap,
beer in hand, demanding, "Tell me
your coming-of-age story," I listened
to the crickets, their clippy curdles
wobbling into the brainspace
between what I thought
could be and
the close evening air surrounding.
He laughed, delighted,
and smiling spoke, "Darlin',
I think I'm still living it;
can't yet tell how it ends."

I can.

He indulged my whim for skinny dipping,
and we lay lakeside on the sloping lawn.
Thinly tented in nylon privacy,
we took flashlight turns reading to each other
Heller's *Catch-22* like we knew what it meant
to love.

New skin itches in stretching.

Sometimes, looking back, I see it differently,
as though I'd dived into the mossy water
wearing full-length wool,

a back-buttoning straightjacket dress
and after, could only crawl out onto the grass, panting.
Then winter followed fast.
So, I could either
sit fireside, sodden and dripping,
waiting for spring, or
pry it off, help required, and
lay the thing down
on the lawn of memory,
letting it soak in sun, desiccating,
or cut and run
underwear-free, knitting new coverings
when I could, lighter this time, linen maybe,
learning first
how to hold the needles.
In the end, by some trick of fate,
converging timelines, or
invisible fumbling paws of naïveté,
I managed all three outcomes
impossibly, as if the wool had a will,
a mind of its own, and still

for almost a decade, daydreams
would scratch obsessive:
Would he be able to forgive
Yossarian and me, both deserters,
as though we still mattered,
as though his forgiveness or mine
wasn't something sparking fear,
more loss, severed thread?

In the end, it wasn't until we met
again, unexpectedly, and ten years after
our last taxi-cab parting
that I allowed myself to see God
shimmering between us
with her honeycomb breath
and the hand she'd had,
had always had,
in bringing us here
together, once more, to say
goodbye, perhaps,
to each other or
to old outfits, our longings
worn brittle by weather
or at least me to mine.

Since I had discovered
what it is to love
myself—the fierce, lonely, wild way
of choosing life
in friendship with the past—all of it,
holding its old ghosts'
torn baggage and bad manners,
not in contempt but a gentle embrace
that makes room for doubt
and sorrow and the terror of possibility
as the uncomfortable but necessary partners
to presence, most precious,

such as was with me
in my shock at seeing him
after all those silent years
that evening in the dim pocket bar
upstairs from the concert
where he'd been one-night hired
as extra security.
It was summer again
and I was wearing shorts
and something sleeveless, and
across the smallest table
I kept my eyes on his elbow
attached to the hand that lifted his glass
while we spoke peripherally
of work and dogs and the city and nodded
from a polite distance,
the air between us tingling.

E V E R Y H E R E N O W

It is a different game
than the one you thought
you were playing
when this is the discovery:

There's none to be had

of what it is
you want, feel
is necessary.

You end
at the end of your limbs
and the borders are kept
by skin, hair, and nails:
short-lived.

The dreams are loamy:
how it is
chock-full
of failure, how it is
fecund
with promise.

How is it
that life shows up
at your door,

a dirty dog dropping fur
weeds, clods, and prickles,
and asks to be
let in?

There may only be this
and only for a little while:
your lights-out pulse
and the wheels of your thoughts
circling the event-
uality of a sleep
that might hold your mind
until the readiness, or
ready or not,
it is time
to wake up
because it is here
waiting
for you, your everyday work
of the heart.

III

THE GAME

ALL DOGS ARE WILD

Small things can be hidden more
or less safely—a life in miniature
> behind glass.

Underground, thirty inches of soil
are enough cover from nuclear fallout:
> old mammal habits

like proliferation are ragged rafts—
inherited, disintegrating.
> I've come apart

to be sewn together, bone-in humor
disremembered, floating feet, falling
> like the leash

from my hands when animal instincts flash
flood the skull, and my soul soars in exhilaration
> and horror

as the dog takes off, calling down doom
> on the squirrel.

DESCENDING WORK

Her wrists end in tatters,
shredded black fans flapping
above her sable skirt
long and wind-whipped
as she courts the dark clouds,
following on their heels,
rolling inward and funneling down
from the sky.

I am afraid of her,
that she doesn't fear
the wild weather
and its threats,
at how she is thrilled
to be both
alive
and only an angel's breath away
from her lover,
that netherworld apparition
whom she came to
dance with
across our dreams,
mine and hers.

The children crowd in at the windows
for a glimpse
of her mutilated elegance,

afraid of neither
the storm nor the woman's steady gait
toward the house
where they ignore admonitions
to cellar-climb to safety.

She has seen them:
how the three main veins
of poison purple the skin
to flower into pressed ash
at the throat and
replacing fingers with clotted petals
curling in, limp and crisped,
and how, when each are upward pulled,
lifted like the honeysuckle stigma
backward through the style,
dragging with it the clear bead,
they are an offering
to the moon
who tucks the trailing filaments,
the blackened blossoms
behind her ear,
past the rim of her rounded body,
visible to invisible,
to rest in shadow,
the far side a quieted place
border-paced by sentinels
of her bright face, by her vision

which now beams
pointing fingers of moonlight,
two palms pooling, silvering
into a working model,
a dual-handed gift
for night work,
for peering into dreams
where the treadmill of transition, travel,
rolling, sliding, swerving,
urgent searching
for a place to crouch,
a tidy cave for laboring,
for crying out and calling in
soul to new life,
whose howls echo
the mutual surprise
of coming to be
here at all

into vision
where the stain on the wall
is the height of a child's hands
and seeps from behind, greasy
with accusation, with suspicion
of foul play in the muddy shape
of murderous intent
and ghostly horror,
an unspoken story,
a hot buzzing hive, a nest
of hair and memory clippings

where the life keeps going,
the eggs hatch, wings flap, honey tracks
in hexagon hiding places
that will whisper awake
whomever is still sleeping.

WHEN THE PREDATOR IS ON YOUR HEELS
THIS IS HOW
TO STALK HIM IN HIS DREAMS

*

"Lake Mead: Shrinking Reservoir Reveals More Human Remains"—BBC
News, May 9, 2022
"[Women's Reproductive] Doctors Face A Difficult Choice: To Flee or
Not"—Texas Monthly, May 9, 2022
"Over Half of U.S. in Drought as Wildfires Burn, Tornado Activity
Surges"—NBC News, May 9, 2022

*

Every
>   *body*
>> *knows*
that rape produces
rage.

*

Here is what happens:
You dam the river, pooling it
for pleasure, meting out its energy
to a trickle, to harness for your purpose
and call it utility.
But we who have bivouacked
in the place that was flooded

are watching your will evaporate
from the desiccated flesh of the desert,
whose exhale uncovers the human remains,
bodies tossed into the water
you thought forgotten,
but this earth will not
hold your secrets
anymore.

*

Why are you astonished
when we would set ourselves afire
to evict you
and your proclivities
to claim, cultivate, plow, and plunder?
The vigil we keep will witness this, too:
the end
to bedrock
where your pits will crisp in
on themselves,
smoking.

*

The other night
when my lover's lips made pilgrimage
to the headwaters
of life, to the underground spring
whispering a delicate prayer of praise,

all of a sudden
I knew this to be the place you crave
to control, the place of power
inhabited by the wild animal
that you fear
with such terror,
that you would word-snare

with statutes and charges,
enlisting your soul-starved allies
feebly perched among piles
of stray letters they add to their names
after exchanging paper handshakes.

I saw how you would
civil-suit-up-lock-and-key
arrest and imprison it,
and once trapped,
strangle and slice:
dismemberment.

But you are strategizing poorly
with your own member-
ship, club hierarchy that betrays
your error:
how you assume power
must be bestowed
from above, must be grasped
from where it hangs
outside of yourself.

This is what you fear,

severance,
and why
you wield swords, scissors,
codified rights
to try to cut us off
from our bodies,
from choice,
because this would be
your worst
nightmare.

*

You are wrong.

*

It has already happened,
the thing you fear
reliving
in the dark,
in the place from which you came,
where you were made
helpless

and then left
alone.

*

While you sleep,
you will catch the scent
of what is waiting for you
to discover
what we already know,
what has been secreted:
the sum of the surveillance
of the eyes of death,

a vigorous pulsing
deep within, beyond sight
or scope's reach,
that groans with a velocity
blood-red and unstanchable,
pouring forth its issuance
past all stoppering-handed efforts.
It is raging, unregulated, feral
with sinew and skin,
limb and desire,
free
to exist
and expire

*

of its own accord.

*

This birth
will come for you
without any blade.
It is an envelope
of death, and it will shroud you,
bewildering your senses
and startling you awake
before you can grasp
what comes after,
again and again and again
and again—

*

how it is
all
that remains.

DEAR AUNT LIZ,

You told me once that you dreamed
of taking out your father's teeth
with a baseball bat. Me too.

I once tied them up,
him and his wife, to wicker-seat chairs, and kicked
them off the end of a pier—any nearby would suffice—
watched them drown, open-mouthed and staring.
Another time, I wrote him into a windowless prison
(since his cash bribe in life ensured that the jury wouldn't)
and fed him paint chips to peel off his skin with
counter-cruelty. It's a shame
he died denying
what we've all been living with: that legacy
of broken-glass gloves, glued on, too-tight
tissue disintegration,
surgeries and scars. His cancer of will
we bear in our bodies.

It's ugly, isn't it?
Thank you for letting me
say what I need to. You always did
tell the truth. Even when it was costly,
you counted the coins carefully: career
connections, public opinion, parents, inheritance,
all a paltry price
for integrity, your daughter's safety, life

uncompromised
by family shams, shadows, and lies.

We've come far in a single generation, yours
absent of males. Bleached bones, marrowless,
hide nothing. You and you sister both chose
desert landscapes for cover
from the blanketing dread of musty walls watching
after-bath rub-downs, not optional,
had your children
endure lidless, unshaded high noons
and "surprises" like birthday parties
or piñatas' spilling which sweets, a Spanish-import
cultural custom we traded up for
abandoning the Deep South's dripping secrets—
sage and saguaro and buffalo grass
more honest about where the water goes and
where it comes from.

I'll tell you what
I saw the other day, grown
woman wandering around in my mind:
a manhole cover, tarnished brass
with heavy engravings, Paleolithic and
indecipherable.
Underneath there was darkness, and within
I reached, unafraid, not even a little
squeamish, though what my hands found
was hideous: a bundled-up rag
of a doll, caramel-colored, resin-stained

once-person dangling long, flat, sleeve-like limbs,
oily and faceless, ragged and panting
like a wheezing lung. It was mine,
somehow precious to me, a museum artifact
begging to be held.
I dipped in again, rummaging, knowing
more had been hidden ages ago,
and pulling up this time a pellet
browned, hard, crystalline-ridged calcium,
maybe, and proteins and blood. It fit
in the palm of my hand, size
and shape of my heart.
Last—and by then, I knew
what I'd find, forgotten I'd placed
there, whenever that was—I brought up
the torso:
headless, though necked and mannequin heavy,
friendly, though stiff, not resistant
to extraction. I gathered them up in my arms,
these relics of me, and with my last savage strength
wrenched from the ground the coppery-brass
round-nosed hollow tube bullet
from its nestling hole, spongy earth fast flooding
with viscous blood welling
up from below, seeping puddles around toes
and soon soaking back in
to an atrial wall yielding to the pressure of my feet,
footprints squelching softly.

What is required now for reanimation
other than assembly? What wind
or whose breath
could abrade the stone's sharp edges,
inflate the limp linen sheathing, empty,
inspire starfish-like limb regeneration, and how much
would it hurt?

I know these aren't answers an aunt has,
but psychology says to ask it of the self,
and her hands are quite busy
carrying the dug-up vestiges of psyche,
and God's been awful silent on this matter
like all the others, so I'm asking you just in case
you know,

since you knew what to say and to whom
when it mattered. I'm not talking about
the police or protective services, attorneys
or judges when you testified in that crooked court
of law—though I'm glad you did, the first in generations
to say anything out loud, and for us girls. I mean
your record-keeping, the truth you told
yourself, kept
for us:
newspaper clippings, transcripts, sympathy
cards and letters of support, diary entries
logging our words, bowel movements, fearful
mid-night wakings, stuffed animals we whimpered for
when we couldn't sleep

in our own beds, crawling into yours
after we spoke
his crimes with our words,
then, surprised to still be alive, cartwheeling
in between freedom from the old crawling hands and
dread of how his hammer had been, till then
and who knew, now, inevitable.

Others forgot, shredded evidence—
myself included. My mother
still won't remember. So one more time:
Thank you, and don't forget
to tell me, when you find out,
how to make oneself whole again,
afterward.

IF THE SHOE FITS

My mother is the heel,
elevated above ground,
detached, shaped for floating
and adrift ever since the scissors
had their way with the leather
or cord, both.
    My grandfather
with his lust for children
is gently pushing
himself into place
as the toe box
and sole.
    My lover-beloved, the last
one I let into my dreams,
gone, recurring, could always be
tonguing his way up
the tanned hide, front
of the loafer, moccasin, mule,
slippery thing
    of fear
and pleasure and sorrow
and longing.
    Here,
try this on, let me
hug your ankle with it,
thumbing your arch
and sweeping the floor

between your knees
with my curtain of hair
hiding my eyes.

*

The shame lies
in the foot bed, the
place of full extension
of the swinging hip,
point of contact
with the path
interrupted,
protecting
the soft pink skin
from the perils of unshod walking.

I want you to wear these.
I want you to carry me.

*

This morning I woke having said, "Stay
away," to that old lover,
the one whose veiny forearms
feel fresh under my fingers
every time I dream him up,
the one with the triangle
of unstoppable power
between his temples and lips,
the voice with the words
to undo me.

I told him, "No,
you can't be here, I cannot
do this again," peeling back
the tongue from the toe box.

Do you know
what it is like
to rip seams
from the fabric
of the universe?

*

Tell me
something
about you.

*

It's midnight already,
and my eyes keep closing
in on these images
of the rocks on the trails
up the Guadalupe Mountains.
My mind goes
to when I lent you my dry socks
after eight miles in a desert downpour
and my sandals were wobbly at best.

In what I see
at the end of this poem
someone is barefoot,
there is blood, and
it must be mine.

FIRST RESPONDER

Upside down and under
acrid odor of oily gasoline,
dark rainbow pooling,
reflecting clatters of the shattered glass
tangling in her hair, she tries
to count the cracks in the asphalt
inches from her face, identify
how many stones and fine-dust aggregates
and how she got here, tasting blood,
seatbelt-hanging feet-up-head-down,
eerie silence louding against the sound
of her rushing pulse, hot temples,
when

      past twilight, empty road-going,
you found her:
ditched Jeep out of place, of shape, bent
close with concern,
reached out your hand,
firm fingers and smooth skin,
the touch

      I still remember
releasing her from the summing trance,
holding her
steady with your gaze
until the sounds of sirens signaled

you both were safe to let go
of this moment.

        Did you,
and how often, return to the scene,
number the heartbeats of your memory
and wonder if you had been heroic
enough, or would have been
if you'd stayed longer, said
something else? What did you tell her
after all? That she would be all right?
Was she?
        I think you were

                a hero
unquestionably,
hands and knees meeting her loneliness
and fear with your answering kindness,
delivered clinging to the cord
of your integrity intact, titanium.
This is true. I love you
for that night now,

             even as then, when
you came home to me brimming
with the story,
I curled up, shrinking
away, unable to ask how you were, say
much of anything, least the
"brave hero lover" to your face

like I knew I should, wanted to, could
only flail pitifully between
your dark-navy-blue sheets
beside your adrenaline-coursed body,
trying to believe I wasn't living
in an upturned wreck
helplessly alone, with you
off saving someone else.

ARTEMIS AS A MOTHER

Maybe she was raped,
her "NO" blown out
like a candle,
and then maybe she said yes
to what can come after.
She knew exactly
how many moons
her body would wax full
before being torn apart,
bringing in
the uninvited thing
living and unasked for.

Or perhaps it was abandoned—
the baby—like small things are,
left on her doorstep,
and something sparked
along her spine
between her empty womb,
her owl-sighted eyes,
and her bow-holding hands
with which she bent
the moonlight
around the basket, leaning
to lift it up, the infant
a voluntary action.

Did she know what would be lost
—or at least postponed
for the requisite number
of blood-moon showings,
however many
years or lifetimes—
her cult of distant devotion,
cool night air,
lung rushing
the forest floor at midnight
worshipping her tawny soles,
and the aloof communion
with her deer and wolves
under woodland stars?

Does she tell her daughter
to prize virginity
as she did her own,
knowing now how fragile,
thin-threaded,
such states of mind
and bodies are?

And does her daughter
see her
longing, keening
into the dark
when she supposes
her household to be sleeping?
And how do either of them—

woman, goddess, girl—
forgive the past
for losing itself
in the shared quiet
hearthside mornings
saturated with scents of oily skin
and impatience,
belonging to them both?

I wonder in what month
or year of mothering
did she, great lady
of the hunt,
lay down her weapon
of forward-facing time,
arrows of freedom and future,
and learn to love
the sitting, holding, waiting
for her daughter,
for herself,
welcoming the truth
that the precious,
most tender
side of loss
is in the letting it
be what it is,
is in the letting
go.

CHOPPED SPICE

The hands and feet, for sure,
were in there,
had been
blood-drained, preserved
whole, ham bone in, skin on.
They were cool to the touch
and still pliable,
body parts of a set
which maybe included forearms
and ankles thumping around
in the drawstring black burlap sack
dragged across the peeling plank floor
and hefted up
beside the tub.
But it was you
who lay in the cedar
half log-sawn barrel
filled with cool water,
a couple of old Styrofoam floes
bobbing amid petroleum rainbows,
and the memory of moonlight
down here
in this windowless basement.

It must've been some sister spell work;
Pythia or Sappho would know
why we were there

together in the dark,
denuded of our fear
and me leaning over
your bare legs
to stir, swirl around the severed hands
like bath salts or laundry soap or
soup, stew, a brew
of newt's eye, frog's tongue,
curiosity,
courage

to recognize
the pink-coral rose
ringing the third finger
on one of the debodied hands.
They are my mother's,
those
that had stroked my temples,
held the tissue to my nose.
I knew those smooth, oval nails
and soft-petaled knuckles,
the uncurled palm offering
itself
into the water
along with the other limbs.

When I reached in
and touched your skin
you moaned, "Please."

In dreams, I'm aware
that each figure is a stand-in
for one side of the psyche, self,
so here is this:
the sharp edge
of transference.
But

when you lead me
away from your breasts, back
to the triangle
of pleasure,
power, and shame,
something inside me squeezes,
pops, crisp
like a blueberry
between the teeth.

EDIBLE EVERYTHING

Yes, you may
bite me, yes, please,
as long as you don't leave
a mark, even though
the ants don't
ask permission and
the swollen skin
on my left arch
twists with blistering
evidence
of the pinchering jaws
that my feet, bared in the grass,
can't say no to,
and now I am noticing
how this itching intensity
draws my attention
down my leg
to pause, crossing
the territory
where your teeth
have made claim
grazing my ankle
before my "Yes" and then
"You can bite
harder
if you want."

The body is
insatiable.

Following, I find
a craving for gravity,
so I go again
to the gym
for more weight,
heavy deadlifts, squats,
pushing shoulder to overhead
so
the whoosh is what happens,
loud rush red
so my body will squeeze
breath from my ribs
to hear heart pounding,
to keep myself grounded
since
my blood seems unanchored
and buoyant, an arterial animacy
clogged up with jumping spiders,
my whole body trying
to fly away, back
to keep playing
with yours.

Please
hold me close
to the bone.

Bring it, send it on over,

the heel-bruising

four-on-the-floor,

the stomping and clapping,

snaps, slap, tumble,

tug and tickle,

like the mosquito

and her exquisite attention

to plunging in

her proboscis

among the feathering capillaries,

nosing her thirst

past my trembling skin

to within, beneath, deeply

partaking

of my body

an unoffered banquet

of liquid life.

Yes, yes,

we might as well

participate

even if it means

being eaten.

Far up

above the city,

the dead

maple leaves drop,

swirl, brushing my cheek,

their light strikes nestling
in the length of my hair
like my fingers knotting
deep to the knuckles
in clover,
tangling turf grass,
grasping and pulling
the way I let you
and lean in, the way I want
your palms
to keep pressing
my neck
long after I've left.

Plus, there's the red-brown,
fox-coat-colored dust
I gently brush
at your inner eye from the fall
along the bridge
of your nose,
around the orbital bone,
right up to the lashes,
and you holding still
your need
to blink, the breath
in the chest synced
with anticipation
of a shadowed sight
for something new
and familiar, both

in a gaze, this one touch.

The room to the ceiling
to roofless sky
is thick with it:
the humming hunger
of living.

The mosquito, too,
like you,
gifts me her imprint,
lasting sensation,
delicious itch:
mementos
of moving through.

When I slow down
enough
in the neighborhood park
and peel back the lids
on experience,
opening both of mine,
I meet a dragonfly's
five eyes, compound gaze
to 28,000
points of perspective—
holy focus.

I don't know how it happens:
When I return, the shelves and surfaces
in my home having populated
with pumpkins,
skeletons and ghosts,
and meanwhile life and beyond
devours me, us, it, all
from the inside out—
smoke in the lungs to
burps in the belly
and branches scratching the shoulder,
birdsong and crickets,
liquid chirping
poured straight
into the skull,
and the breeze
through the window that sees
and seizes the senses, sparking
awareness
of an eternal
invitation.

So
shall we
dine?

THE ONES YOU NEVER WANTED

Some gifts arrive darkly,
not on the doorstep
with the ring of the bell
but as a splinter,
soft-tissue embedded
deep within,
between the knotted yarn
balls of the hips
and the watchful sockets
within the paper pelvic wings
enfolding the holiest
of holies, where a dry crackling
of a bow drill
echoes in a scapular scraping.
The splinter will work its way
in from the wooden stake, meat peg
your limp body was hung on.

These are the gifts
that are close to the bone,
the ones that, to accept,
you must
begin singing
in the dark
alone with the wound.

Sometimes, in the other room,
the dog howls in his sleep.
Sometimes you wake
from yours, still barking
into the shadows.

It is your voice
that knits sinews
and pours the synovial fluid,
the longing,
that holds together
the skeleton in the night.

It is a long work
and you will tire, sorrowing,
waiting for sunrise.
Your voice will become hoarse,
croaking.
You will wonder,
What is the point?
When will it end?
You will approach the edge
of despair
with this throaty thrush song
raking your windpipe,
and you will
keep singing.

Your limbs will move
of their own accord
in time
with the rhythm
of your strident breath,
close and hot in the dark,
and your muscles will ache,
sprouting damp twisting tendrils
that quilt themselves across your torso,
filling each mucosal cavity
with membranous secretions,
with desire,
and you will know you are
singing flesh
onto these bones.

It is a long work,
one chilled and sweaty,
and the splinter—
glass shard, shrapnel—
will keep working
its way through new flesh
that is pink and raw and raging,
tender and swollen,
and when it surfaces,
emerging, glinting
with some moon
or starlight,
you will recognize it
in the predawn glow

on the horizon
of your body's memory
as the gift: silvery,
sharp,
and irrefutably
beautiful.

SUMMER HOLIDAY

At forty miles an hour,
towing a trailer,
Black Canyon Road, no shoulder,
there is no swerving
for the cottontail
who dashes out, heading straight
on its path across, curtailed
by the tire. In the SUV, the impact
is almost imperceptible.
It is my dismay that registers
in the instant sighted, white flash,
split-second inevitability
just before,
and its twitching
trembling reflection
as I drive away, moving fast,
so fast.

Later:
It is a cool morning, the 4th of July,
outside of Durango, or maybe Pagosa Springs,
where townspeople and tourists
dot the fresh-cut lawn,
tickling from canopy to awning,
milling, congregating, celebrating
the memory of collective independence.
I see her majesty,

the deer,

turning her head high, alert.

I think I have learned

from the rabbit, so I slow

enough to see that she is lying

roadside, broken,

at least one leg twisted beneath her,

and she will not

get up again.

I do not stop.

What can I do?

These things happen.

There are fault lines in families.

We mirror the fractured surface of the Earth.

Seismic shifts happen:

the divergent drop

of the head through the birth canal,

a marriage transforms,

the loss of a parent

is perpetual subduction,

and we can almost hear

the scraping plunge of the deep dive, one layer

of the heart

beneath another, and suddenly

the landscape is foreign,

the ground between us

unrecognizable.

Sometimes we are the driver
and sometimes we are the doe,
the tire, the asphalt, the spirit arrested
in grief and hovering to linger
with the life
going out of the body
as it does, in the end.

After the earthquake, eruption, strike-slip collision
when all is changed,
and the shadows here are new shadows
on the now-unfamiliar shape at our feet,
I lay this blessing, promise

I will not leave you,
will not get lost as a ghost in memory
longing for what no longer is, searching
for the time before.

Together we will hold it,
what we loved
and no longer have,
hold it
in the reverence
of gratitude
for having been, for being
on the road
at all and
open to what
there is.

FULL CIRCLE

Bright as the bluebonnet
or wild sage,
my father's veins
would wobble, rolling
between my tiny pressing fingertips
and waving like buffalo grass
on the wide plains,
the backs of his hands.

The smallest, innermost
of the nesting dolls
is within, watching
from the hillside of the heart mound,
where she grows
limbing and sprouting,
swelling and rooting,
in fear and admiration
of herself
like the magnolia
waxy in the moonlight.

The stars were hiding
behind the floodlights
when, one night at halftime
as a child, I went after my mother
who, down the steps and out of sight,
I found in the crowd

by the sound of her
clearing her throat, scarved and all.

We are animals, still.

Here is the landscape:
Like the limestone cliffs or copper breaks,
the crumbling Earth splits,
revealing her arteries,
a weathered story running into the past
long beyond memory, sparking
in the sun.
I am astonished
that now, after all,
you shoulder the gathered supplies
and walk with me, keeping pace
on the snowy trail,
sweaty and chilled and weary,
and later,
in low-hanging starlight,
let me press my skin to yours
so I can hear our thudding pulses
close. Breathing your air
is almost as good
as your voice in my ear—
"I'm listening, I'm here"—
while you hold me, and knowing it
will be true tomorrow, too.

IV
FIELD DRESSING

FOR YOU, POPPA

The day I decided to stop complaining,
my jaw fell clean off its hinge,
a white bone clattering
straight down to the matching caliche.
My tongue rolled out
a far, flat road,
a pale radish peel
endlessly ribboning itself,
highway straight to horizon.

On it, somewhere between the Brazos
and Lake Diversion,
three hundred swallows are diving
from their thatched baskets,
each with one dark round doorway,
and all of those honeycombing homes
nest on the underside of the concrete lip
of the farm-to-market overpass.

Here,
I am mud
beneath the lake,
subject
to sun and winds and plastic pieces.
I am dry and thirsty and drowning
in contract with the season's
way-making with my surfaces.

Here, I am that fading repulsion
to the odor of the body
where I am feral, all claws
and hunger.

I might as well hold you,
womb-becoming in the darkness, both
your mother and granddaughter,
molecular lover
shapeshifting your gods
in my person.

Together we will hold
the two who fell from between my legs
and the three who died before they could, and
beaked and winged
beyond each threshold,
we will teach the babies, all of them,
what we know with needle and thread
and what we are still learning
with slow words and slow walking
these asphalt-bandaged lands:
how to migratory fly,
everywhere and always
dancing.

LAMENT FOR COLONY COLLAPSE

By our hands and our silence
they are stunned,
confused flapping
and failing to find their way
back home where the queen cares
for the young, still innocent
and unaware
of the combs coming down
around them, empty
and mirroring their brothers'
blank eyes and human devices
crafted to kill
pests (bad luck),
and this only a byproduct.

We have lost so many
bees, miracle fliers,
that now they are mythic,
a story we tell
to our grandchildren
how, once, their mother grew
pumpkin vines from seed
and the bumblers visited,
blessing the orange star flowers
and our sight.

In all the true stories
there is a leak,
hole in the boat, but
instead of water infilling,
from punctured raft
the air is outseeping,
sapping the nutrients
spaded by too-eager exploration
or blind-eye denial, or both,
of the vascular wounds
in the flooded stalk, and beneath
where the roots have been
loosening hope.

There is no stopping it, no
clotting process, no
caulking the cracks or pitching
the hold, and only by letting go
of this illusion
can we sorrow
as we are called to.

Because, like bees before us,
our senses confused,
toxin-maxed into madness
topped with fear,
we forget how
woe will make way
if we let it, paving a return home
on the dogged breath

of the living.
Quick!
Before it's too late.
Take this tonic, benediction,
recalling gently the touch
of the mind and heart,
these gifts of grief and silence
in which soft words may blossom
between us for the hearing,
and may, out of the haze
of this dreamless deep sleep,
life reawaken within.

DEAR SONYA C—,

Thank God you rolled in when you did,
full-blazing tidal bore,
brandishing forgotten field hollers
bare-handed like flaming swords,
and bringing in psalms and work songs
to your desk corner next to mine,
only one hollow-block wall away
from where the state inmates—
wearing white so their stains can't hide—
were waiting for your migratory landing,
waiting like I didn't even know
I had been, to hear you rebuke
the crime of punishment
for cruelty's sake,

like when the law took up all their radios
and started writing cases for contraband,
tore up what few family photos and
confiscated dignity, tried to
keep optimism hostage.
And the boys all went berserk,
started flooding the runs like God himself
would bother to trouble the water,
and you, just
there, steady, calmly
handing out star-chart spirituals,
pointing northward and quietly

humming "Go Down Moses" in harmony
with the five-man extraction team.
Yours was a call-and-response
that had meaning.

For me it was a maze in there,
shifting sands,
West Texas dust
gritting up wired-shut
windows and razor-like labyrinth
campaigns propping up
crooked ladders with crumbling rings.
And before you rolled in, I was blind
to it all, lost without a string
and my eyes on the shuffling feet
scuffing out poor excuses,
making small bets, smaller talk
into my hands
as if they or I or anyone nearby
could be satisfactorily
flayed and scarred
or granted that "well-earned earthly resolution"
Nietzsche once called freedom. No,
no,
but it was only after

you showed me how
to get on board
underground
that I began to understand

we carry our own
spikes and rails
and trust the ties
are already there.

Girl, I know you had to go,

but you left too soon,
flew homeward before I could
tell you this: You were my deus
ex machina, proof of miracle
not even Horace could criticize.

FOR THE VULTURES

Sometimes the old city unfolds itself
like a map,
and I can move across it
with my fingers outside of time
or let my feet carry me
like a specter through the ghostly streets
that, nearly solid,
taste of curry and car exhaust,
of fried meat and pho
and the wind off the lake.

And unexpectedly
I'll meet old friends or,
more often, my last lover
in a bookstore or a bar,
recognizing the longing
of things unsaid between us,
skirting through the threads
running knotted and sticky
like spiderwebs woven
to countertops or foosball tables,
implements as foreign
to this dreamscape
as the language
we once had for each other.

Waking startled in the dark,
there are only the dogs to hear
my muttering, a desperate prayer:

May regret be banished
to the realm of sleeping stillborns
where womb's unspoken memory
knits new life
alongside old echoes
when it must,
as it does.

We know not everything
conceived lives to breathe,
and yet the lost welcome us
when we visit, tenderly
bestowing wreaths of fragrant pine
and of presence
—theirs, or ours—
in the whispered space
between this tight-sewn stitch
and the next.

We need not fear
the stooped birds, either:
They are not harbingers of our final ending
or doom and decay.
Their intimacy with death
has always been double-sided,
a compact with life

winging skyward, cycle long forgotten.
Dear buzzards:
Here, take from me
these words and dreams
born lifeless of the wound
and transform them with your dignity,
condor soaring above us all
on the wind off the lake
against the bright emptiness.

AT THE CAVERNS WITH SCOUT TROOP 575

The cave-swallow preference
for the forked ribbon-end tail,
and the diving and gliding
and daylight hours
kept enough
of the colony, flock, patrol
back at camp,
done with venturing for the day
to scrub dishes
and full-moon gab

so that only some of the others—
most of the women but
all of the mothers of daughters—
setting out just before sunset
saw it,
what we had come for,
answering as pilgrims
a call beyond hearing
to witness

the vortex-swirling release:
these rising shadows
flitting against the cavern wall,
cliffs bespeckled
by the yucca and prickly pear,
onlookers to this thrill, these

shadows, sacred shadows
with a pulse
and teats and milk and menses,
teeth and migratory momentum,
the bats will ride the earth's exhale
with winged instinct
into night

above the budding ocotillo
with her red-tinted tips
not yet open to the season, and
the Lechuguilla and Adam's needle
and the Texas mountain laurel
throwing her candied scent
down before us,
above the sage and buffalograss,
flying, following the promise
that the Rattlesnake Spring across the ridge
is wet enough to quench the thirst
of constant flight
in a sky bejeweling itself
until dawn

when
the return journey
home
to the embrace of First Mother,
beneath and within
what we dim-light don't see:
how they rest

among each other's breath,
alive in silent rhythm
and invisible sounding calls
that paint their way.

This return
holds our hope,
our initiation
into seeing
ourselves, who we are
in this dark
protected space,
who we are at the borderline
sentineled around and ushered in
to and from above below
poised, hovering, flapping,
embodied and
liminal,
becoming
this paradox
of an ancient memory,
a sunset yawning
always into longing
for knowing
what's yet to come.

When we return to camp,
we say, "Ten thousand," in response
to "How many?" asked by those who stayed,
as if this question could hold

for them some justice
in their choice,
as if anything other
than the moment
of startled reverence
for the wild twilight flight
in its stark, denuded wonder
would serve the fire of conversation
around this night gift:
an encounter marvelous
enough to dream
and wake by.

CLOSE TO WORLD PEACE

Do you remember
when the earth stood still,
silent, the animals
tiptoeing back into the cities,
the air clearing into visions
forgotten
of mountaintops for miles
after our pollution fog fled
only a few days in
to the crowning pause,
breath and movement hushed?
I remember, too,

how the heat started rolling in
on 100-degree days, 110, one
after the other after
the other, sauntering, sizzling,
and hospitals filling up
again
with friends and grandparents,
yours and hers and his
cousin who had the bad heart
and her niece with diabetes
and thank goodness the kids
will be fine (probably),
so let's go ahead and open the schools
where they won't be touched,

not even a little,
while rhetoric continues on
spew-raging,
darkening the skies,
and bodies keep moving restless
into danger and saying,
"Such is life."

Last year,
when my friends came to visit,
we took paddleboards
to the canyon lakes
at dawn
because even those months ago,
days got hot quick,
and I remember
the trash-snagged
shoreline caught
bottlecaps nesting in the reeds,
plastic smashed into the mud
lapped by lazy water.

That morning my hands
gathered every misplaced scrap
my eyes could see
through stinging tears and
the lopsided wingbeats of my heart
thudding angrily, desperately
flicking the tatters of hope,
and then

I climbed aboard and floated
to where the current was stronger,
breeze in my ear, and I waved
to them standing beneath the trees
that were.

I guess I mean this
to be some small morsel
of atonement,
performative speech act,
my *I do*,
a thousand cranes
rising into our air
sorrowing
the five billion birds
pushed out by our habits
encroaching
onto their homes.

Regrets?

Whatever they are
have been inherited
on this slopeside scramble
directionless,
and I woke here clawing at the dirt.
This was no willing descent,
but transformation
needs no motive,
so I take up

this new soundless flight
myself, reclaiming
the innocence first
that has always been
redeemed and waiting
for us all,
and then the arms
strong enough for striking
and holding us together: you
and your fear, and me
and mine.

DEAR DOUGLAS B—,
(After Adrienne Rich's "Translations")

I apologize for using your name, hers;
you aren't her, despite the heirloom,
so let me start over:

Dear Mother, mine,
we don't have to talk
about bad seeds since your family had several
snakes in the grass we all fell prey to
without shelter from catapulting fruit
falling rotten off the original tree,
its knowledge of the evil
you seem keen to keep forgetting.

I recall
that after you left, I looked for you,
catching occasional will-o'-the-wisp glimpses
within the kind gestures of kindergarten teachers;
in my own mind, hearing the lore
of your sister's mother-hen pecking,
how she drew blood
from shallow roots, unearthing lies,
pulling up sickly ivy,
the limp version of our family tree,
she a pullet-winner in the cockfight;
or

in my first husband, your sturdier reflection
I was too afraid to face.

So mostly I found your absence, my loss
hollow inside, collapsed vein, dry riverbed
sloping predictably down,
seduced into embracing the enemy:
despair, claiming *prima nocta* eternal.

Until sorrow showed up with my ransom.

She combed my hair softly, soothingly,
whispering sadness-streaked tales
of courage like yours—
moments before *conceptus*, mine. How wonderful
was your negligence,
deciding it was safe
enough to let my father into that dark place
which must've felt cavernous with echoes,
the voices of fear and pleasure, duty and allegiance,
confusion crumbling louder than thunder—
I have no idea how loud
anything else could have been to drown it out—
forgoing your own fingers' climb
in at the swollen entrance
up the spongy wall, already moist with desire,
to omit some fumbling fitting
of the cervical cap, silly silicone sailor's hat,
would-be barrier to my life.
Your courage to allow it, that

desultory joy
that spasmed me, in his sperm, up
through your oven to the pink pipe where I,
single cell, half, had traveled and was already
there, waiting to join, be made
whole.

(By the way, I'm sorry
I never got a chance to deliver, with you,
your vagina at my birth,
as my daughters did mine,
passing through it, at theirs.
You and I missed it,
that singular opportunity
for redemption. I'm sorry
that the doctor—of course he was
a man—chose for us, denying me passage,
wrenching me out your womb's side door,
surgical escape hatch,
incising your use-scar once again.)

I try now to reckon tenderly,
how garden gone, and I growing up in a desert.
I think you tried
to water me when you could
remember,
and it felt as though you did
often look upon with love,
sunshine-kiss sometimes, your seedling, me,
mostly strong and healthy, free

of the disease,
the plague disinherited
and even flowering now and then.

ON BEING HELD

The baby's cries come in
to the canvas-and-mesh
tent perched
atop the car I'd overlanded
into the Sacramento Mountains
one weekend: late March, still snowy,
the narrow valley crowded
with waving pine needles
and the sounds of the waterfall
and the emptying
of the child's lungs
into stillness.

Maybe other campers, pilgrims,
were traveling toward sleep,
but even then, how could they
ignore that infant call?
My own heart thuds
a parallel protest,
primal greeting,
"Yes!" in answer
erupting from within,
breath steaming, "Yes!
Cry!" I say into the dark, the air,
ice crystallizing
around our voices.

It is hard!
This life, this cold, cold night,
and I equipped
to embrace myself
with eiderdown and fleece,
a woman's body
holding the memory—
enough memories—
of how to survive
the star-glanced mountain air,
the tail end of winter,
and still I shiver here.
"Yes!" shouts the waterfall,
echoing between my tent
and the other, where
the infant howls
loudly, wholly,
as it knows how.

It is not the same
baby as the one
who sleeps within my dreams,
nested among the pressing wings
surrounding it: blue-black
iridescent sheen
and ingrown
to the nursling's flesh and muscle, sewn
somehow while they all slumber,
the babe and the birds,
thirty eyes

closed to the cave
where I found them, within,
closed to the world without.

One time, I tried to save her,
reached to take her
once,
the baby in the dream deep
within the grotto,
and only once:
the wing-screaming flaps,
the crowing protests,
the wide-eyed fear
of the child
who had been
peaceful sleeping
until then, and who
drifted back, lulled
into easy-seeming rest
as soon as I let go.
I don't know why
she is there, flocked
and held
by beaked black protectors.
I do not know what
she wants or how long
she'll stay or
when, in what next night,
I'll gain admission
to her presence

dark and holy.
But
I know she is not sad,
is not alone,
does not cry out
into the cold
or hungry or tired spaces
anymore.
She has not had to
since the ravens heard her
call, most desperate,
and came
the first time.

I think of her, here
at the equinox, nearly spring,
early in the camping season.
"Yes," I whisper again
later, when I am finally warm
enough to rest. "Yes,"
I say into the frigid air
between us,
me and that child,
alive
to whatever spirit
has drawn its parents
and me both
to the forest this night
where we share the starlight
and the pine scent and fir

over a riverbed and the sound
of falling water, and
I hear also
the faint rustling
of feathers.

CATHARTES AURA

Some times, like this morning
sleep withdraws itself
before 4 am, and though I am practiced
in waiting, it doesn't
return.
So I resign
myself to this:
the bald-headed committee
in the back of my brain
and its watching,
with an occasional hiss,
the deft work of my hands
with the water
and strainer and herbs—
some ritual to bring back
me to myself.
But then they all start shifting
one foot to another, feathers ruffling
and red-raw throats cawing
when they see
the kettle.
The word sparks their wild
memory, and then they won't let go
of this poem.

Their animal shadow
is one lean and hunching,

shrugging awake to the threat
advancing on tilted horizon,
and when it approaches
as predators do,
the vulture sends out
from its depths
the deep bone-encoded
instinct to spew
up
through gullet and gizzard
whatever it has, half-eaten
meat, putrefying.

After all, this is only
survival.

The wings spread wide
on the updrafts in flight—
have you seen it?

When your business is alchemy,
transformation,
what is your pleasure?
And I wonder
about its beak immersed in decay;
how does the stiffening muscle,
sulfurous soft tissue
smell up close to a nose
that can scavenge for scents
at lengths more than a mile?

Far back enough—that is, hundreds
of millions of years—
there was one
common ancestor
to us both, a mother maybe,
before the branch split between
this body and the bird's
and surely she knew
better,
but now we believe in
the sins of our fathers
demanding redemption,
a slate-cleaning, scrubbed,
polished, pure, clamoring
for this growth-gripping crescendo
so far beyond trusting, out of touch
with the endings, the downfall,
expiry
and also
again, of the rise
on the thermals
off the river's arms
sturdy with washing
and holding the land,
off the mountain's shoulders
late afternoon-draped
in piñon and sage.

Re-member me to this:
the kettle, these birds, ourselves

together
on the frictioning air,
to the smashed rotting scent
drawing us close
to the site of impact
of plastic and metal and burnt
flesh and petroleum
left on the road, now molten asphalt.

Yes, let's find a way
to the pause
in the last sacrament
of inert matter
that life left, took flight from,
in the born-again baptism
of urine down the legs
where we compose together
in the wake of the inevitable
and become this holy casket
where death is
a part
of endless renewal.

ARTEMIS'S DAUGHTER

Her arrival
changes the story:
a revision
between
the known
and what goes unsaid.

In greetings
her jaw is tight, heavy
with the words she tries to speak
and cannot, clenched
around the memory
of what she has said, ghosts
falling from her mouth
invisible, unheard.

Her hands are nimble,
deft fingers stretching sinew
and braiding flax fibers.
She holds her first bow
long before she first bleeds.

And when she was younger,
much, much younger,
her fingers would float, lifting
to her mother's face,
pulling on the jawbone

to tilt, bring in
her mother's
attention
on the axis
so that she could tiptoe-peer
into her mother's eyes,
so her mother would
look back.

She is older now and
cozy enough with the concept
of cycling that she sees it
clearly. Her mother's moon eyes
go out of focus,
vacant gaze, drifting apart
and taking her somewhere
else.
She has learned,
as good daughters do,
to let it
alone.

She does not know it
(How could she?)
that she is the eclipse,
and in her own shadow,
in secret, she begins
digging, seeding, coaxing
the night phlox and nettle
she has found budding
in herself.

What she does know
is that she is
also
the sorrow
and the songbird
both.

FOR THE CAESARIAN-BORNS

Held
in the dark, in the starless night,
weightless and tethered
to life itself,
we did not ask for it,
the slicing of seamless deep space,
the searing of atomic light
shredding reality.

We did not ask
to be pulled, tugged, dragged
by the head or the ankle or arse
into gravity, stunned
at our limbs' heaviness, how we were
white-glove handled and electrified
by our first draft of desert air,
a double-lung recoil,
and yet
this is our story.

And so we arrived
as womb-longing wanderers
chasing dreams and dragons
into dark corners we almost recognized,
every precipice an invitation,
straddling the infinite crevasse
and daring to look down,

catapulting our anger
far above ourselves
and grappling-hooking our desperation
to get ahead
of our bodies, of our surprise,
to hijack time
with our demands
to be ready.

Here,
an invitation
to pull your knees in close.
Let these few words weave
silk, spin the blessing spell
to chrysalize fast-hatching memories
in alchemic secrets: the truth
that you are both
the one within, waiting
to awaken, to announce
your ripe intent,
timely arrival, triumphant,

and also
you are the one without
waiting, too,
in joyful confidence
of your own "yes,"
your decision
to join the long dance
of push-pull, scream-sing,

tearful laughter
inevitable
at your final surrender
to the wind,
where the breath of life
will dry-rustle your wings
in welcome
to a new kind of life.

SAYING GOODBYES

the day i decided to stop feeling
sorry for myself,
all of my innocence
gathered itself up
into a mushroom cloud
and seeded the atmosphere
with vapor dreams
of the soft lie: "you can have
what you want."
as if unbuttoning the impulse
that points itself toward comfort
would, denuded, not be
what it is, ever
the elusive invitation.

as though this pile of lost baby teeth
could ever stop wanting
candy.

the groaning sound
the throat makes with the mouth
or the heart or the knees
at the work,
always at hand—you know, that
phone call, laundry, or toilet scrubbing,
or saying "no"
and walking away

from the unwelcome thing,
the work that needs doing
regardless
of the creaking sighing
bearing-down skin-splitting
tearing fabric,

involuntary
noise, is the same one
that nut shells and seed pods
soil-bound in spring
fling into worm shit.
it's heard by no one,
the cracking
that has to happen,
the willingness
to let through
the sprout.

V

FEASTING

IMPACT

Last night, we were at the football game
where the lights at full volume
went loping wildly around the concrete stadium,
colliding in fractals of cheering voices,
and through the crowded fog of bodies
        all of a sudden
I saw soft muscle trembling
in every eyelid and brow, across the mouths
of the ticket holders, there for sport, and
like the vase-or-two-faces illusion,
the distance between the spectators
—subtracting scarves and jackets and hats,
layers against the indifferent air—
solidified. Wavering mirages took shape
between one shoulder and another and the next,
as animal bodies between us each
crouched, rippling and poised
for springing contact.

After I slipped my hand into your pocket,
you brought out my gloves.
I looked up, discovering
your temple above the ear
and its estuary lines
branching toward the eye.
You caught me staring, didn't you?

In bed this morning, the old fear surfaces
as it sometimes does—what if
we're not two today, intruded on
by unpleasant images, childish memories,
an unwelcome third wheel rolling in, but then
your fingers comb the inlets at my shores
and a curtain draws back in my mind, and I know
every tender touch between us
is innocent,
an infant dream
startlingly remembered
of skin and breath and thudding heartbeat,
warm and safe, and
of being held.

SALMON RUN

Sweetheart, please do
take all the time
you need
to grow into your skin.
You are an unfolding
process to be honored;
I will wait for
what else is there
for us
to do, you
or me, either.

In the summers,
when the heat and pressure
are like a rock tumbler,
collision friction abrasion
polishing the bones,
I used to make some
innocent pilgrimage
to the fish ladders
and hatcheries
stair-stepping up
and open tank laid out
for the public.
I would come with pencils
and journals, ready to record
the phenomena, to call it mine.

I was carrying fistfuls
of expectation
and somehow
it was never the season,
and the water behind the glass
empty.

Now I see
it may have been
an invitation
to travel deeper
into the old-growth forests
hugging the curves
of the shorelines,
to let the leaf's lament
leaving the chlorophyll to be
the brittle crisping signal
and invitation to a new season,
to wait.

This question, laid out
for the lover:
Will you bear it?
The weight
of the heavy eyelids,
the waiting, the load
of letting be, the waiting,
the holding
time and your own desires
for warmth

in the chilling October air
and watch, camped out there
beside the stream bank shallows
with an eye to cascading course
for as long as it takes
to witness
the lithe body,
all muscle and slippery motion,
forward-thrust
up the churning fall,
primary leaping efficiency.

The longing is to cleave.

It is the morning star who whispers
to the girl who asks for help
in The Seven Ravens' tale.
It is she who, in the near dark, conjures
up a gift
in her silverly doubling way
after ushering in the evening
some stack of moments before.
The crooked bone she presents
will click in the lock's hinge;
and when it's lost,
as it must be,
is this question:
How long will you hesitate
before doing what must
be done?

After all, the girl should know
how to use a knife,
and we are all handed
more than one
of these keys
at the end of each of our arms.

And sometimes,
between each twilight
in the stillness and the dark,
the blood seeps through
the bandage, my dreams of you
a lengthening thread, raveling
on the blackberry bramble
and pricked with the sensation
of the weeping distance
that your river trips
must have been full
of sights of salmon.

And that is true, but
so is this: You are worth
everything, and

we are bound
to hold this
here, between us:

I my self
and you,
yours.

SING IT IN YOUR CAR, I'LL DANCE IT IN MY KITCHEN

If you bring them, your
lacewings and feathers,
costumes of desire
whorled and twisted aestivations
in their tightly curled buds,
the needles and spines
on your skin and its milkblood
and serums, your humming and hooks,

I will, too,
unfold the storm veil,
heirloom quilt bundling
the patchwork memory
that is my story
and lay it here next to yours
on this saltwater altar
of a porous velocity
leaking rain between us
and flooding the pact
between time and gravity—
the only one
that always seems to be
happening.

I want to fall
with you

from the smallest tower
whose brick increments
are only grains of sand
and the sensation of falling
still palpable, but
only barely, and
at the end
of every exhale.

The sun is slanting
on the south slope now.
With our shadows pointing north,
let's mark these moments
of silence and speaking,
however many months
of passed scribblings,
whatever lifetime of longing
we've each borne or buried
or both, to show up here,
tipping into the darkening season
again together
with this
precipitous sigh:
thank you thank you thank you
thankyou thankyou thankyou
thankyouthankyouthankyou
thank

MAKING LOVE

The girl will beckon
from the corn flowers,
shouting an opening line
electric
into the air between you
where scents of blue thunder
unravel
your longing
like her braided hair
coming undone
in the sunshine, day doing
what she does
now turning, teasing
you to follow.

She is young and easy
to catch hold of,
but when you do
she will leave her body
smoking.

You will travel in circles
many times over
around the sun, and even then,
after so much star travel
so long,
you will be fortunate

if you find her,
the woman.

You will know her
by her standing
outside her home, broom in hand
and chest forward, friendly
with the weather, whatever
it is, and she will
whisper you close to hearing
her invitation
to remove your shoes and come
within
where she, sovereign, keeps a fire
lighted and a basin filled
for washing and an oven
warm with morsel gifts
for your arrival
because she knows
in her heels and thigh
bones, bound sinews,
the road you've traveled
and its weary-making.

These are her ways,
and she will hold you
if you let her,
and you do not even have to
stay, but she would like you to
look beyond

your longing
to heart-sight, take into
yourself
her
kind of knowing
what is to be done
and doing so.

A POEM FOR THE DARK

Darling,
I would like to meet you
at the place where words fall
to their knees, ankles giving way,
their right angles unraveling,
stem to tail and flourish;

the place at the evaporative edge
where language is only just
a steamy memory of warmth,
and nothing to say and nothing
to be said;

and where words aren't matter
probably mouths don't either,
but in my mind I bring bread,
a loaf or so for sharing
in case the journey's long,
though distance would collapse there, too,
wouldn't measure much
besides being
a concept

like this one:
If my fingers can find each other
in the dark, then so can we,
wordless, superfluous, unspeaking;

like this one:
You already know
what I need to tell you need to hear
about everything and nothing more
than being loved and about love
and how you have always been
and how you are.

THANKSGIVING SONG

This is how it happens
for me:
You've sporulated
with your loving silence
into my lungs, alveoli
the best of messengers,
runners to the blood, and
I draw you in,

only you
are a carven tree, dogwood
horse at the gates of Troy,
host to paradox
of size, impossibility,
God contained within you,
and I am contaminated
by grace.

I wonder about you,
how your feet feel
within your socks
crossing the hardwood floor,
how your hips move—
your femoral head
socket-swiveling as you stand
from sitting,
the lilt of vibrations

humming in your throat,
a sound ivy-climbing down
the ribbed house of your lungs
and heart.

I want to be the rose
petals spiraling
around your stem.
I want to stay
awake here
for you, in case
you look up.

And when my longing leaf-turns
in the wind and falls
as the inevitable
truthful tears
of that familiar loneliness,
the sad-eyed guest
who never speaks
will leak the world
from her sighing.

Then I know
my blood is branching
with the white serum
of your spores
which, anyway, you would say
are God's,
and really,

it doesn't matter
because their fruiting bodies
along the long vines of my sinew
hum with the same flavor
of your loving silence,
alchemized between us
into a spongy song,
sweet nectar of something
beyond
you
and me, something
divine and deserving
of everything—all praise
and this
joyful obedience.

SOMETIMES I JUST WANT TO SIT ON YOUR FACE,

and not just as a way to wake up
to my body, not just
to carbonate my chi
or whatever
it is that gets me giggling,
tickled from the inside out,

but also because I like the idea
of a tesseract,
the supposedly impossible
meeting of places:

this, my softest, most secret region,
a mysterious threshold
well worn in its crossings
of moontides and blossomings and
the entrance to life
and all the comings and greetings and
griefs,   and
the place where
your body forms language—
yes, your efficient staccato
of bullseye aims
these arrows,
but as they leave your lips
become only words, after all.

I'd cover them
with the upward-tenting shelter
of my seat,
shadowing your vision
with fleshy proximity,
lowering as much of my
spread-wide hip-socket weight
against your skull as it takes
to relieve your mind of its worry—
that lifelong running script,
the background accountant
with the cool gleam in its eye—

with my hands on your chest,
my fingers ribcage wandering.
If you wanted me to, I could,
I like to imagine,
pin you to a different perspective

beneath the holy well
between my legs
and water you,
because some rivers of life
taste like salt and sweat
and you could chant
an ommmmmmm
that would go spiraling up my spine
and disintegrate

the tiny gnawing endless tasks
like always needing to be
filling the car with gas
and remembering to pay electric bills
or setting the alarm for Saturday chores

and even the needling
questions about enough
and having or being it
would melt into the pelt of gratitude
worn by my breath, clear in your ears,
and you could see yourself
here, supine, and me, erect
above you, with you, and we
together
a momentary lightning rod
for pleasure
in the middle of it all.

YES, YES, YES, PLEASE.

Here, darling,
is where I want to call you
closer in
than skin,
although there, too, we could touch,
if you like. Here, beyond
the tongue at the teeth,
soft palate, into the lungs
within the ribcage, our bodies
clumsy with my desire
for you
to be my bubbling blood, for me
to be your breath
passing the lips.
I want
to be your impulse
to inhale and
the relief you feel
in sighing, lying
back
here with me.

This whole world is wild
with longing:

the acorns rushing
into gravity's arms,

the old rosebush rising
up onto her elbows, putting out
her last lascivious petals
of blood-purple blooms
before tonight's freeze,
a dog barking, music
filtering over fences,
squash bugs and their eggs
everywhere.

The pulse of desire
is palpable
even in
this thin November light.

Maybe it's the falling temperatures,
the crispy frost on the grass,
that video of the first snow
in the mountains,
but whatever it is, it sparks
in me a push,
a pilot light for the season,
marrow warmed.

I want
to see your eyes.
I want you
to want it
with me.

I just do.

Here
is how I try to tell you:
A peeled pomegranate,
fruit leather from my oven,
your favorite meal,
the raw egg yolk separating
from the white between my fingertips,
folding laundry late afternoon,
inviting you into
a poem, maybe,
words
disfigured by desire,
chucked into the abyss
between what I mean
and what happens
here, in the place
of exiled titans
where I want
everything.

Don't
do
anything. Will you
just want with me?
Keep saying it, whispering
especially to yourself
some version
of

the "YES,
I want
to be
here."

EPIPHANY

When the men arrive
as friends
of your husband,
as houseguests,
they come bearing gifts,
their longings
clear and netted
with solitude
and the hope
that guides travelers
home.

They tell stories
of themselves,
what it is like to live alone,
how to spin myth
from desire and dread,
their stories unfolding across the table,
one uncertain glance,
chance meetings of a mutual gaze,
one cup, one sip at a time
of tea and whiskey and laughter
long past moonrise, early
into morning.

They are generous in sharing
meals and memories,

notes on an old instrument,
fears of what may come
unknown and looming,
and the miracle they have not forgotten:
how to play
games with your children,
their aging ears ringing with the noise
of giggles and shouts and cheers,
of small soles slapping
the cold floor underfoot.

Before they depart,
returning to whatever life
of prayer and loving and laboring,
wandering, listening, forgetting,
or single-bulbed scribbling
they left for this
brief pilgrimage,
they will walk across the water
of your dreams,
hovering above your sleeping body
slack and soft, unguarded
below the winking eye of night
which watches
how you receive them, hosting
your questions and
opinions of yourself
in the mirror of their eyes.

*

There is a hallway with many doors.
Within a magnolia grove, late afternoon,
a fire ring and tent pad, weedy with years.
Transit-card timing, a panicked scan,
and so many stairs up to the platform.
Hotels, elevators, breath in your ear,
a gondola approaching
an indoor swimming pool
you don't have the fob for
and the maps, timetables,
papers and tickets,
always tickets, and at last
the asking:

What have they come for?
Why do we travel
if not to behold
one another, if not to be held?

*

You wake,
hearing the houseguests stirring.
You wonder
what can you do
but tell them they're welcome,
as if a pallet and pillow,
sheets and a towel
and coffee and conversation
might be enough,

as if it will
hold,
so you do.

DRAWING BACK THE VEIL

i. grief

What to do with this dead animal?
Its limp tongue dry on my wrist,
lolling head, vacant stare,
bare teeth underneath floppy lips
agape, still warm.

Silky coat and soft body, someone
handed it to me. I think
its bowels are leaking,
the only movement in death.
Or did I kill it? Guilt

whispers that I might atone
by taking it to sleep with me, wearing it
draped around my neck.
After all, it's soft enough.
Almost beautiful.

Embarrassing, though. I can never shake
hands (obviously) while it rests
safely behind my back, clutched.
So I seem a schoolgirl, neatly pleated
lines. I hope it doesn't smell

like loss, like tragedy: dead giveaways.
Speaking difficult with this onionskin tongue
peeling away. I squeak, "I'm sorry,"
and the animal's eyeball mirrors
spit back, "Of course you are."

Maybe someday I'll set it down,
sweet pet, discover a plot
beneath the pine trees perhaps.
Cairn-cover it, tenderly, and redeem
the heart buried where the animal should be.

ii. how to collude in family secrets

To place blame squarely
is a lie

when it is shaped more like a whip
in the hands of a petulant child.

Cheek slashings, unapologizing,
it is a landslide, flash flood

slot canyoning hearts of stone into
layers, narrowly banked,

carving up with gravity and erosion
scarred fault lines.

It is lightning
flaying the fingers, unwieldy saber.

It is an electric arc
burning saltwater-painted paper,

splintering fractured spindly crevices
off the main artery.

You give it the slip,
and I'll be the rod.

iii. incantations for coming of age

At eight:
Crisp up the carpet in the front living room,
nylon Berber loops blacken
in an expanding circle
of horror. Lucky if your father is close
enough next door, ready to help and hold
you accountable for unchecked fascination,
for his negligence.

Sixteen:
Discover why open flame is required
for crafting curses, how in utterance,
candlesputtering "I love you" is simple,
plain cruelty when you don't mean it.
Truth is relative. Now snuff out
any lingering doubt about
whether you can do it. You can.

Twenty-four:
Last lesson in causinomancy:
Figure out how to use
first love for firewood, kisskindling
longing into conflagration.
Go ahead and char the rest of your trust
in yourself.

Grab hold. This is powerful magic,
transforming what matters
to a piped payout:
mouthfuls of ashes and eyefuls of smoke,
nothing leftover.

iv. on whether you can "fake it 'til you make it"

The short answer is "probably," although
it gets a bit complicated. Maybe "maybe"
is a safer bet to speak out loud, especially
to someone else. Because it takes longer than you think,

like the slivers of a shattered femur, splintless,
groping their way back toward each other.
Or a muscle-deep gash, gaping flesh
unsewn, sans debridement, knitting new layers,
swollen and weeping exudate.

                          Meanwhile, smile.
Because more dishes are involved than expected—
vacuuming, alarms chiming, clothing changes,
shedding bedsheets, double wash loads, gasoline
refills, paystubs, bills, fifteenths of April,
and so on.

              You are the earth, your heart the coal.
How much pressure can you bear?

You have to believe it will work, too.
And the balance between faith
in ersatz, stockpiled, hunkering-behind-hope-
in-a-future-self-fed-mainly-facsimile-dreams
and delusion is delicate, slight, dangerous.

This is all assuming, of course, that your vision-making
mechanism for deciding *what to fake*
has fared better than the femur.

v. liability

The holes are filled now
with composite resin,
a gift from
my parents
who could afford better
than amalgam,
and from dentistry,
which had already ditched
mercury and lead.

So I got powdered glass and plastic
in the mouth he'd stuffed with candy,
clamping my lips around it, locking
my jaw while looking me in the eye.

Mom and Dad, conscientious,
took care of the teeth problem
with trips to the dentist:
grotesque attempt to amend
the cavernous damage.
But they should know
latex smell and laughing gas
hardly count as an apology
for a lazy eye, inattentive,
for a preoccupation
with insurance coverage.

Nitrous oxide instead unmasks
the dread of opening,
of the prodding and pointy tools
I am expected to host
every six months.

One cavity was redone twice,
and it still needles on contact
with tortilla chips, piercing,
with almonds supposed
to be healthy, and
with the unexpected bite
of cereal not quite soggy
so that no menu is completely safe.

My souvenir.

vi. Saline Flush

I know what it is to be lonely,
to be turned out
of my own heart
splat, landing on a rib step
while above, the inverted organ
pulses grotesquely, muculent
pools of dimly lit drips rippling
with the aortic valve constricting,
cut off from the lungs.
I have seen enough blood
spurting from self-injury,
heard enough—enough!—
apophatic relief
contorted
around adrenaline's coattails
flapping like the open vein
incised in obeisance to despair.

But what if we found out
how gravity works on the soul? What if this
discovery is muddier than unearthing
fossils, and what if recovering
is more meticulous than channeling
alluvial plains, the wait
on rainwater interminable
and notwithstanding
this obsession with –covering?

How we geocache our secrets,
hide them in gray-matter folds,
try bloodletting for divination,
map and GPS out of sight, in hand.

And I know there's no explaining how,
but look, still rib-step stoop-sitting.
I stumbled upon it and
resolved to begin it
again, this beatbox
rhythm, cupped palms looking up
to where my heart, collapsed
and spongy, inside out, eyed my
pale envelope of skin and sinew,
loose-knit cradling new self-
uncovered truth: that we can
catch our breath together.

And so it did, secreting tears
warm and hemoglobulous, inhaling
me home and pluripotent again,
complete with compass.

I'll tell you again if you ask me.

WHEN MY THERAPIST HINTS AT THE VIRTUES OF HOPELESSNESS

i take to writing
this one poem
which is, like all the others,
a line thrown
at the center, carrying waves
rippling thinly out,
thrown from the hand's
attempts on meaning
toward
the second person singular
from this undersea place
where anemones course
up damaged dendrites,
particles poised and buffered
among katabatic winds,
flying off the echoing mountains
and tumbling down
through to the prairie
grasses where i've hidden
the roots of some dark hope.

who knows what
was speaking through the voice
of the skinny, white-girl yogi
wearing tie-dye sweats and standing
in front of the windows

filtering light
into the matted rectangular class
on st. patrick's day in lubbock, texas,
as she mystically intoned
that there are forty thousand neurons
dancing
around the heart.
                    i heard
the crackling air, i lay there
imagining an ocean
shorelining tidepools
in the center of my chest
until a black cavity opened up
in the lower-left ventricle
and deep within it, wrapped
in wrinkled brown paper,
a small pile of baby teeth
silently clattered, asking
to be found, to be
held,
probably
cherished,
i guess, because
what else would they,
could they possibly want
from me?

forty thousand neurons
that love to ache.

anyway, i know you
have these spells
where something descends—
a veil, shroud, cloud,
misty and soporific,
with the opposite of desire
the polar other end
of motivation, and
you're down for the count,
a few days maybe.

look, we all have our demons.

last week, walking
around the playa lake,
i saw three blue jays
crowning the branches
of an elm. this week
the geese are gone
again north, and
(i wonder if they flew over you)
there are white blossoms
on the pear trees and
new shoots already greening
a coy watchful place
for the sharp-eyed
feathery chirpers, spring royalty,
and i below
notice,
let them

be, these
papery petals that unfold
in proximal space
to my reach, but not quite
there,
and then breeze
blows
and then
they go.

indoors, the yellow dog at my feet
drops half her fur
in vortices of the softest needles
like a pine-straw blanket
carpeting the kitchen tile.
she passes nearly every test
of loyalty, of belonging,
especially against the fedex drivers
and the solar-panel salesmen,
but if i let her look me
too long in the eye,
she loses it, snapping,
lips peeled back and lunging
for my face.

the last time i didn't
hear from you... what was it?
forty-eight hours? maybe seventy-two?
so few in a tooth's
lifetime but more

than what it takes
to panic, than what makes
whatever halo happens to hold
those neurons
in orbit around the innermost muscle
turn on themselves, turn
into a tightening lasso,
a tourniquet, threatening
to sever an arm of the starfish
that has taken up lodging
in the sandy organ
brimming with saltwater
between my ribs.

i don't want to lose you
like i lost the others.

the electric charge
around my heart
has always known why
the dog will snap and lunge
as though she could snatch
for herself
forever
what she sees in my eyes,
as though she could tear out
my attention.

now
i can,
do
make this promise:
i will be human
for you, me,
us both.

darling,
i can't promise
it doesn't hurt
because what the hell
are we
doing here, anyway,
besides allowing
life to roll us over,
letting
god the process
have its way
with us, like the season
does with the blue jays
and the blossoms,
like the flurrying fur with the floor.

tonight i am asking my dreams,
nighttime soothsayers,
to assemble the baby teeth
and let them speak
for themselves.

in the heavy limbed darkness,
i find
they are quieter than expected,
holding half-circle space
for the blade of the tongue
to rest softly behind them,
trailing the sibilant hiss
and the first-light L
at the top of their back:
"listen."
as if it's enough
(that it is, because
it must be)
to say nothing at all,
to shut up, lovingly,
to roll up these lines,
and like i must do with the geese,
let you
go.